D1505810

Career Discovery

Careers If You Like Animals

Toney Allman

ReferencePoint Press®

San Diego, CA

About the Author
Toney Allman holds degrees from Ohio State University and the University of Hawaii. She currently lives in Virginia, where she enjoys a rural lifestyle as well as researching and writing about a variety of topics for students.

Picture Credits
Cover: iStockphoto/Fotoedu
 9: © PAP Photos/Photoshot
18: iStockphoto/Kali9
48: Associated Press
64: iStockphoto/Roberto David

© 2018 ReferencePoint Press, Inc.
Printed in the United States

For more information, contact:
ReferencePoint Press, Inc.
PO Box 27779
San Diego, CA 92198
www.ReferencePointPress.com

LIBRARY OF CONGRESS CATALOGING-IN-PUBLICATION DATA

Name: Allman, Toney, author.
Title: Careers If You Like Animals/by Toney Allman.
Description: San Diego, CA: ReferencePoint Press, Inc., 2018. | Series: Career Discovery | Audience: Grade 9 to 12. | Includes bibliographical references and index. |
Identifiers: LCCN 2017007634 (print) | LCCN 2017022129 (ebook) | ISBN 9781682821350 (eBook) | ISBN 9781682821343 (hardback)
Subjects: LCSH: Animal specialists—Vocational guidance—Juvenile literature.
Classification: LCC SF80 (ebook) | LCC SF80 .A54 2018 (print) | DDC 636.0023--dc23
LC record available at https://lccn.loc.gov/2017007634

CONTENTS

Introduction: For the Love of Animals

On a farm in Wake Forest, North Carolina, Molly Goldston is fulfilling her dream. She is the founder and executive director of a nonprofit rescue organization called Saving Grace Animals for Adoption. With the help of a small staff and a group of volunteers, Goldston's organization rescues dogs from overcrowded animal shelters, where many are euthanized every day because there is no room for them. Goldston often drives hundreds of miles each week to find animals whose time is running out—she hopes to be able to give them a second chance. She rehabilitates the animals, provides them with necessary medical care, spays or neuters them, and lovingly cares for them until an adoptive family can be found. It is a job that only a person with a lifelong passion for animals could do.

In college, Goldston majored in business management and marketing to prepare herself for the practical side of running a rescue operation. Then she worked for the Society for the Prevention of Cruelty to Animals (SPCA) to learn all she could about animal rescue needs. Finally, in 2004 she was able to establish Saving Grace. She doesn't care that she is not on a typical career track for financial success. She measures her success in lives saved. "A day in the life of Saving Grace is long," she says, "but the moments are full of hard work and endless hope."[1]

Goldston struggles with the sadness of leaving good dogs behind in a shelter because she has no room for them. She must also cope with the day-to-day drudgery involved in caring for sixty to eighty dogs at one time. No matter how inspiring and glamorous her career may appear to others, she emphasizes that hard work, community outreach, and just plain mess are as much a part of the job as loving dogs. For instance, she often has dog poop on her shoes or spends her time cleaning up diarrhea and vomit. She also must engage in continual fund-raising efforts and work to teach people that rescue dogs make great family pets. She sticks with her organization year after year because, as she explains, despite everything, "the dogs turned out to be my saving grace. . . . [I witness] the power of love and value of life each and every day . . . I still love it!"[2]

Multiple Careers, Options, and Skills

Goldston turned her love of animals into a career running a highly respected and successful rescue organization. There are many other ways that a love for animals can translate into an equally rewarding, lifelong career. Some paths require years of formal education, while others call for practical, hands-on experience. Some jobs involve managing domestic animals, and others deal with wild or exotic ones. Some animal careers are about saving lives and protecting animals, while some are about furthering human knowledge and benefiting humanity.

If you like animals, there is an amazing assortment of animal-centered careers available to you. Though they are all different, many share a need for similar personal qualities and skills. First among these, of course, is a love of animals. "We don't go into this profession for the money," says veterinarian Kimberly May. "While the financial rewards can be high, the work itself is rewarding."[3] Without loving working with and helping animals, no amount of financial success could make the career satisfying.

Almost every animal career also requires good social skills, because many of the jobs involve dealing with people. Veterinarians and pet groomers, for example, have to be good at communicating and working with the people who own the animals. Meanwhile, educating the public is a big part of zookeepers' and animal conservationists' jobs. Even academic careers, such as those in biology and zoology, require the ability to communicate with peers, government policy makers, or university administrators.

Other skills necessary in most jobs include scientific ability, some physical capabilities, and having the self-confidence to judge situations and make good decisions. In medically oriented careers, for instance, it is important to understand anatomy. Similarly, studying animal behavior in the wild demands a good grasp of the scientific methods of observation. Physical strength and dexterity are critical for the veterinary technician who has to restrain a frightened animal or draw a blood sample. Conservationists also need these qualities when they, say, need to capture and tag a wild hawk without causing injury or getting hurt themselves. Finally, since animals can't talk, those who work with them must be able to assess conditions, develop treatment plans, identify needs, and use their own judgment about what works best for the animals. In addition, sometimes animals suffer and die, so people with animal careers must have the strength to face the stress and sadness that may come with their job. Nevertheless, for those who love animals, the rewards far outweigh the downsides.

Wildlife Rehabilitator

Most of us feel sad and want to help when we come across a wild creature in trouble, but a wildlife rehabilitator doesn't just feel bad. He or she knows what to do. Wildlife rehabilitators feed wild creatures, give them first aid or medical care (under veterinary supervision), and house and care for them until they are ready to live on their own again. Rehabilitators do not try to make pets of their charges. Instead, they hope to free each animal and enable it to live the wild life it was meant to live. The National Wildlife Rehabilitators Association (NWRA) explains, "The goal of wildlife rehabilitation is to provide professional care to sick, injured, and orphaned wild animals so ultimately they can be returned to their natural habitat."[4]

Rehabilitators tend to be needed most in areas where wildlife habitats and human populations intersect. Citizens call on rehabilitators for help or advice when they find an animal in need. Or public officials notify a rehabilitator when such an animal has been found. Although many wildlife rehabilitators are volunteers, others have paid positions that involve educating the public about wild animals and helping individual animals return to the wild. If you love wildlife and care about protecting the animals, wildlife rehabilitator may be the right job for you.

What Do Wildlife Rehabilitators Do?

Wildlife rehabilitators often care for orphaned or injured animals, which are kept in cages or pens until they are ready to go back into the wild. A day in the life of a wildlife rehabilitator is not for the squeamish. He or she may have to crush up a frozen mouse in a blender to force-feed an injured hawk. Frozen bloodworms and large and small mealworms are typically fed to other birds. Every wild animal has specific dietary needs, and the rehabilitator has to know and meet those needs for a variety of animals.

Mess, stress, and sometimes injury are also part of the job. A wild animal that is temporarily restrained in an unfamiliar environment is also under considerable stress, and that can mean constant mess. A rehabilitator may have to repeatedly clean a frightened raccoon's pen that is splashed everywhere with diarrhea and vomit. Additionally, wild animals can lash out at the humans who come near them. One wildlife rehabilitator had his hand chomped on by a frightened fox that had gotten tangled in a human's backyard volleyball net.

For wildlife rehabilitators, most days involve preparing meals for feedings, cleaning cages and keeping animals warm and dry, providing needed nursing care, doing laundry and dishes, overseeing any volunteers, and monitoring and keeping good written records for all the animals in their care.

Highs and Lows

Almost all rehabilitators say that the best part of their job is when they get to successfully release a healthy animal into the wild. Julie Anne Collier, who specializes in raptor rehabilitation in Springfield, Massachusetts, knows this feeling. Collier once raised three baby screech owls found abandoned on a roadway. She spent weeks

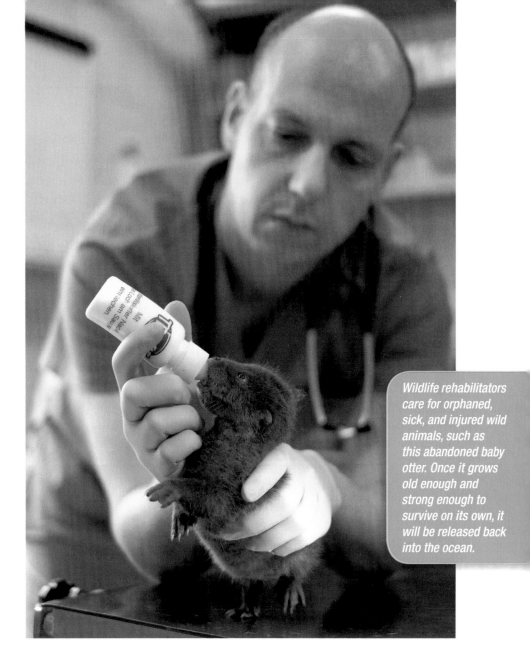

Wildlife rehabilitators care for orphaned, sick, and injured wild animals, such as this abandoned baby otter. Once it grows old enough and strong enough to survive on its own, it will be released back into the ocean.

caring for the little owls, feeding them microwaved mice and using a hand puppet that looked like an owl so the babies would not get too attached to her. She let them learn to fly in one of her large outdoor wire pens. When the owls had grown big enough to be on their own, she let them go in the woods. When a rehabilitation like this is successful, she says, "there is an incredible feeling of release and relief."[5]

However, not all days are like that. Almost all rehabilitators say the worst part of the job is not the long hours of care but having to euthanize an animal that is beyond help or watching an animal die that he or she hoped to save. Amanda Margraves of the Florida Keys Wild Bird Rehabilitation Center explains, "A lot of the animals that we see are very badly injured or very sick and do not survive. Dealing with death so often is a very stressful thing."[6]

A Typical Day on the Job

No matter what kind of wildlife is in need of care, wildlife rehabilitators work hard to accomplish their missions. One such person is Willow Bender, a rehabilitator at the nonprofit Clinic for the Rehabilitation of Wildlife (CROW) in Sanibel Island, Florida. CROW provides veterinary and rehabilitation care to more than two hundred species of wildlife and more than thirty-five hundred animal patients each year. As the senior rehabilitator, Bender works with veterinarians, other support staff members, students, and volunteers.

She begins her day at eight o'clock by making morning rounds of all the patients. Next she prepares morning meals for all the animals and supervises students doing breakfast feedings for orphans housed indoors, such as baby raccoons and opossums.

10

Outside animals are fed in their large enclosures, and each gets appropriate food, such as frozen chicks and mice for birds of prey, berries and mealworms for songbirds, and live shrimp and crabs for otters. The rest of the morning is devoted to cleaning enclosures and pens; washing dishes, towels, and bedding; and checking the animals' weight, behavior, and overall health. By noon Bender is helping with vet checks, wound management, changing bandages, and performing necessary blood work and medical tests.

Bender's favorite animals are the turtles in the clinic. By one o'clock she can be found providing care to turtles that have been hit by cars or are suffering injuries from predators. She takes these patients out for grazing time, lets them bathe in tubs of water, doses them with needed medications, and changes dressings on injured shells. Although it can take months, most of the turtles eventually heal and are released. Around three o'clock each afternoon, turtles and other animals that are ready to go back to the wild are released to appropriate habitats. Bender says, "It's definitely one of the most rewarding parts of the job!"[7]

By four o'clock Bender is back at the clinic, where she supervises dinner prep for every animal and then helps give public education presentations. Some injured animals never recover enough to leave the facility and live there permanently. Bender integrates them into her presentations as wildlife ambassadors. For instance, when she gives talks to visitors at CROW's education center, she lets them interact with a hawk she carries with her.

The last part of Bender's day is devoted to doing final checks of different animals and keeping computer records, in which she updates information for all the clinic's patients. She does not leave the clinic until about seven o'clock. It is a long day, but Bender wouldn't trade her job for anything else.

Volunteering and Getting Licensed

Every local wildlife center or facility needs volunteers, and volunteering is the best way to find out if wildlife rehabilitation is for you. You can gain skills by handling and caring for animals in a wildlife rehabilitation center, being mentored by a rehabilitator who runs a volunteer or nonprofit facility out of his or her home, or volunteering at a zoo, an animal shelter, or with a veterinary practice.

Such practical experience is almost always a requirement for licensing. Wildlife rehabilitators must have the required licenses or permits from the state in which they operate if they are to legally take in orphaned and injured wildlife. Each state requires a rehabilitator to have particular levels of experience and hands-on training. States also require rehabilitators to pass oral or written exams. In addition, those rehabilitators who wish to work with migratory birds need certification and a license from the federal government.

In the state of Virginia, for example, beginners are allowed to apply for a Category 1 permit under the sponsorship of a licensed rehabilitator. At this level, they usually handle orphaned but healthy baby animals. After two years, the Category 1 rehabber may get certified as a Category 2 rehabber, in which case he or she can care for injured animals. Also at this level, the person is eligible to apply for a federal permit to rehabilitate birds. The federal permit mandates that a rehabilitator must have at least one hundred hours of experience and prove that he or she has adequate facilities. Twenty of the one hundred experience hours required for a federal license may be in classes, seminars, and other academic training. It is illegal for anyone to keep in captivity or attempt to rehabilitate wild animals without legal permits.

What Education Do You Need?

In general, wildlife rehabilitators need a minimum of a high school diploma and practical experience. However, there are several advantages to getting a college degree in a related field such as biology, zoology, wildlife management, or conservation. The relevant classes provide knowledge about animal diets and nutrition, anatomy, physical needs, and natural habitats. They teach the rehabber to re-create an environment as natural and appropriate as possible for a wild animal. They provide an overall understanding of conservation issues as they relate to animals and people.

Getting a degree makes it more likely that a rehabilitator will be hired by a wildlife center.

Job Opportunities, Pay, and Future Outlook

Many wildlife rehabilitators work as volunteers or privately from their homes and depend on donations to remain open. Others are able to acquire paid positions in different government agencies (both state and federal), for nonprofit groups and wildlife centers, or at zoos or humane societies.

Wildlife rehabilitation is a labor of love, not a way to get rich. Most paid rehabbers earn from $25,000 to $35,000 per year. Those who have formal degrees and extensive experience can become a manager or director of a wildlife facility, positions that pay average yearly salaries of $51,000 or more.

The NWRA, individual wildlife rehabilitators, and wildlife rescue centers all agree that more rehabilitators are needed. The Bureau of Labor Statistics predicts that jobs for non-farm-animal caretakers (under which wildlife rehabilitators are categorized) will increase approximately 11 percent from 2014 to 2024. Nevertheless,

The Fine Art of Release

"We do our best to return injured 'Birds of Prey' back to their home range, which is within a mile for a few reasons. First, adult birds might have a mate and family they need to rejoin. Second, nature has something called a 'carrying capacity' which essentially equates to a fine balance of all species in which it can support. You shouldn't relocate ANY SPECIES. 1. It's often illegal to do so. 2. It's usually not successful; less than 20% of relocated wildlife will survive."

—Liz Nicholas, wildlife rehabilitator in the North Georgia Mountains

Liz Nicholas, "Day in the Life of a Local Wildlife Rehabilitator," Blue Ridge Highlander. http://theblueridgehighlander.com.

opportunities for paid positions remain limited as yet because financial support is hard to come by for nonprofit wildlife centers.

Find Out More

National Wildlife Rehabilitators Association (NWRA)

NWRA Central Office
2625 Clearwater Rd.
Saint Cloud, MN 56301
website: www.nwrawildlife.org

Most licensed wildlife rehabilitators belong to the NWRA. It has a wealth of information about careers in rehab as well as practical information about wildlife and how to get help if you find an injured or orphaned animal.

Ohio Wildlife Rehabilitators Association (OWRA)

1075 Rte. 343
Yellow Springs, OH 45387
website: www.owra.org

Follow the "Find a Rehabilitator" link on the OWRA website to find a complete, up-to-date listing of certified wildlife rehabilitators by state.

Wildlife Center of Silicon Valley

3027 Penitencia Creek Rd.
San Jose, CA 95132
website: www.wcsv.org

Discover what a real wildlife center is like through photos, articles, and information pages on the center's website.

Wildlife Rehabber

website: http://wildliferehabber.com

Follow the different links for information about wildlife in general, rehabilitation, articles and photos about rehab, and how to find a rehabber in your area.

Veterinarian

A Few Facts

Number of Jobs

About 78,300 as of 2014

Pay

Median income of $88,490 per year

Educational Requirements

Doctor of veterinary medicine degree

Personal Qualities

Love of animals, communication skills, compassion for animals and people, good problem solver, calm in emergencies

Work Settings

Vet clinics and hospitals, laboratories, classrooms, outdoors on farms and ranches

Future Job Outlook

Expected growth of 9 percent from 2014 to 2024; faster than average

Veterinarians may serve in various capacities and specialty areas, such as teaching in veterinary schools or researching new vaccines in government laboratories. In general, though, veterinarians (or vets) are medical doctors for animals. They diagnose and treat diseases and injuries in animals, as well as maintain the health of their charges with preventive vaccines and medicines, dental care, and nutritional prescriptions. Vets educate pet parents and large farm animal owners about animals' needs and medical and behavioral issues. They also provide end-of-life care, including euthanasia, when it becomes necessary.

A vet may care for small animals such as cats and dogs. Or he or she may specialize in the care of horses, work with farm or ranch livestock, provide medical care for exotic or zoo animals, or concentrate on laboratory research. In any setting, veterinarians have an extensive array of knowledge and skills. They can perform general health care, dentistry, surgery, and obstetrics. They can set bone fractures, prescribe medications, and use diagnostic equipment such as X-rays, ultrasound, and microscopes. Just like medical doctors for people, some vets become expert specialists in medical areas such as ophthalmology, cardiology, or emergency and critical care for animals. Given this, veterinarians have a wide variety of career options available.

A Typical Day on the Job

About 75 percent of veterinarians work in private clinics and hospitals and treat pets, which are also called companion animals. As of 2016, approximately one in six vets owned their own practices, while the rest worked in larger practices with other vets. For these vets, a typical day is spent indoors interacting with human clients and their pets in exam rooms. Pet owners' reports and concerns are explored, and the pet itself is directly examined. At least half the day is usually devoted to seeing animals by appointment to do checkups, give vaccinations, diagnose sickness or behavior changes, treat illness, or provide follow-up care for an injury. Frequently, veterinarians reserve half the day for spaying and neutering or other surgical procedures. These tightly scheduled activities, however, can be interrupted at any time by walk-in emergencies.

The Hardest Part

"No matter how long you do this job for, you never get used to having to put animals to sleep. I've been a vet for five years, and it's still very hard to hold back the tears, but I have to remain calm and reassure the owner that they're doing the right thing. And it always is—we'd never put down a healthy animal and that's a huge consolation."

—Alice Duvernois, veterinarian

Quoted in Lorraine Fisher, "A Peek in the Life of a Vet: No Matter How Long You Do This Job for, You Never Get Used to Having to Put Animals to Sleep," *Daily Mail* (London), January 14, 2010. www.dailymail.co.uk.

Dr. Maegan Melillo practices at Clappison Animal Hospital in Waterdown, Ontario, Canada. On a typical day, she is scheduled to do surgeries in the morning and see regular appointments in the afternoon. When she arrives at the hospital at eight o'clock on one particular morning, however, the hospital staff already has an emergency waiting for her. It is a four-year-old Lab mix that has eaten the poison from three rat traps. "I examine the patient, a plan is formed, an estimate is created and my four legged, rat-trap-eating friend is admitted to hospital," says Melillo. "The morning is not going as planned but you just have to roll with it."[8] Finally, by nine thirty, she is able to begin her scheduled surgeries, and there are no more interruptions.

By the beginning of the afternoon, Melillo has time to telephone clients and check on the status of patients that are at home but are still ill. She also calls other clients to report on lab and blood work results from previous visits. By one thirty she is ready to see her regular appointments. She says, "Most appointments are what I would consider to be straight forward, vaccine appointments intermingled with the occasional, and adorable, puppy and kitten appointment."[9]

Then at four thirty another emergency comes in. It is a frantic owner with a dog that has been injured in a fight. Melillo sedates the dog, stitches the wound in his side, and then sends him home with prescriptions for antibiotics and pain medication. By five thirty the doctor can leave the hospital after another satisfying day of caring for animals. She says, "I get home, have a long, hot shower and think to myself, 'I have THE best job' and it is true. A veterinarian's life is not glamorous but they love what they do. They love the animals, they love the people and they love medicine. It's just that simple."[10]

A Different Kind of Day

Dr. Teri Coon loves being a veterinarian, too, but her typical day is quite different from that of a companion animal vet. Coon is a large-animal veterinarian with Agricultural Veterinary Associates

A veterinarian performs an exam on a canine patient. Vets diagnose and treat illnesses and injuries and oversee preventive care for pets, livestock, and even animals in zoos.

in New York State. The veterinary practice serves a multitude of farms spread across several different counties, and Coon spends each workday traveling to the different farms that need veterinary services. Most of her patients are dairy cows, and a big part of Coon's job is helping maintain the health of the herds and monitoring the status of cows. She visits some farms every week, some every month, and some every few months, depending on the size of the herd and the farmer's needs.

In an average day, Coon examines 150 cows to determine whether they are pregnant by sticking her whole arm up the rectum to feel through the wall for the cow's uterus. She checks other cows to see whether they are ready for breeding. She examines any cow or calf that is worrying the farmer because it won't eat or is acting sick. She may also have to perform surgeries right on site. For instance, she may have to stitch up a laceration, repair a hernia, or remove a tumor. "I took out an eyeball back in the spring," she says. "It was disgusting." The cow had a tumor on its eye and was cured after the surgery. As she leaves each farm to travel to the next one on her schedule, Coon disinfects herself and her instruments and changes her clothing and boots. "Even if there's nothing to worry about, you want to wash up and start fresh," she says. "It's just like a doctor washing his hands between patients."[11]

Working Conditions

For a large-animal vet, working conditions are fairly dirty. On farms the environment is likely to feature manure, mud, and animal feed and bedding strewn around. Often there is no protection from the weather, and these veterinarians work during all seasons of the year. They also run the risk of getting injured when, say, a 1,000-pound (454-kg) animal objects to a medical procedure. Coon, for instance, has been kicked a few times but fortunately never suffered more than bruises.

Companion animal vets deal with the possibility of injury, too; animals that are frightened or in pain may bite or scratch. Vets in clinics or hospitals work indoors, but they do work in noisy environments, with animals protesting and many patients and humans awaiting their turn to be seen. Pet owners have to be treated compassionately because they too can be frightened, demanding, or grieving. Pets themselves cannot tell the doctor what is wrong, and they require a gentle but thorough assessment in order to problem solve and diagnose. The testing may involve getting urine

If You Want to Be a Vet, Go for It!

"I hear all the time, 'I thought about being a vet, but when I saw the course load I decided to do something else.' There is no bigger regret in life than not trying something you want to accomplish. You only have one life to live, and it is better to be doing what you love than settling for something just because you thought it would be too hard. Never settle for less than your capabilities. It is amazing what you can accomplish if you just work hard and push through the pain."

—Dr. Kayla Cheek, veterinarian

Quoted in Scientific Minds, "I Heart My Science Career! An Interview with a Veterinarian," August 17, 2016. www.scientificminds.com.

or fecal samples, examining vomit, or cleaning pus from a wound. Much of what a vet does is not pleasant, and when an animal can't be saved or must be euthanized, the job can be very sad.

Nevertheless, vets value and care deeply about animal welfare. For example, Dr. Charles Dolin of the Essex Animal Hospital in Bloomfield, New Jersey, writes, "Yes, there are happy times and sad times, but I practice veterinary medicine with one underlying philosophy, and that is to always do the best thing for the animal. In my mind, the pet comes first, and everything else is a distant second."[12]

What Education Do You Need?

To become a doctor of veterinary medicine, you must graduate from an accredited four-year program in veterinary medicine. To be admitted to a veterinary medical college, most schools require applicants to have a bachelor's degree, preferably with a major that emphasizes the sciences. Courses in chemistry, biology, microbiology, physics, and zoology are typically necessary, along with other science courses, mathematics, and liberal arts.

In addition, vet school applicants must take standardized tests, such as the Graduate Record Examination, to be accepted into a program. Admission to any college of veterinary medicine is competitive, with only one of every three applicants accepted.

After graduating from veterinary medical school, new vets are licensed through a national board examination. Some then go on to practice veterinary medicine immediately, but many choose to complete a one-year internship in a veterinary college or with a vet in a private practice. Those who wish to enter a veterinary specialty (such as oncology or exotic small animal medicine) continue their education through intensive training in a three- or four-year residency program.

Personal Qualities

A successful veterinarian has a passion for animals, compassion both for animals and their human owners, excellent communication skills, and dedication to the profession. He or she must also have good business, organizational, and time-management skills. In addition, the successful vet is good at customer service. He or she treats human clients with a friendly, helpful, professional attitude that helps people feel comfortable and trust that the veterinarian will meet the wants and needs of their beloved pets. Finally, good vets are quick thinking, capable of responding calmly in emergencies, and able to handle their own emotions while supporting the grieving pet parent when an animal dies.

Job Opportunities, Pay, and Future Outlook

Veterinarians are in demand, and job opportunities are excellent, no matter what kind of specialty area or animal interest the vet has. Vets may go into private practice and establish their own clinics, work in an established clinic or hospital with multiple vets, work in a private research laboratory or government facility to improve animal and human health and safety, or even work in a zoo or for a private business as an on-call vet. Income may range from a low of

$53,210 (usually for newly licensed vets) to an average of $158,260 for the top 10 percent (specialists or well-established vets).

Demand for veterinarians is predicted to grow faster than average when compared to other occupations. The Bureau of Labor Statistics predicts a 9 percent growth rate from 2014 to 2024.

Find Out More

American Veterinary Medical Association (AVMA)

1931 N. Meacham Rd., Suite 100
Schaumburg, IL 60173
website: www.avma.org

More than eighty-eight thousand veterinarians belong to and are represented by the nonprofit AVMA. On its website, interested professionals and the public can learn about the latest news and research in veterinary medicine. It also provides a database for identifying current clinical trials for animals with various conditions.

Association of American Veterinary Medical Colleges (AAVMC)

655 K St. NW, Suite 725
Washington, DC 20001
website: www.aavmc.org

With a large section for students and those interested in applying to vet schools, the AAVMC's website offers much information about preparing for and achieving a veterinary career.

Department of Veterinary and Biomedical Sciences

College of Agricultural Sciences, Penn State University
115 Henning Building
University Park, PA 16802
website: http://vbs.psu.edu

Penn State University offers a major in veterinary and biomedical sciences for pre-veterinary students at the undergraduate level. The mission of the program is to prepare students for veterinary school or graduate school. At the website, the College of Agricultural Sciences provides extensive information about admissions, courses, and the steps to take to become a veterinarian.

Dr. Patty Khuly
Sunset Animal Clinic
8776 Sunset Dr.
Miami, FL 33173
website: www.drpattykhuly.com

Dr. Patty Khuly is a veterinarian, author, and pet advocate who has penned numerous articles and columns and provides occasional posts on her *Dolittler* blog online, describing the real world of veterinary medicine. All of her interesting and enjoyable writings can be accessed at her website.

Veterinary Technician

Veterinary technicians are more commonly and casually called "vet techs," but many vets, such as Dr. Marty Becker, call them "the unsung heroes of animal care."[13] Becker explains that vet techs are the nurses of animal medicine. Under the supervision of a licensed veterinarian, vet techs can take temperatures, insert IVs, give vaccinations, draw blood, clean teeth, dress wounds, and monitor anesthesia during surgery. They take care of many of the technical duties involved in an animal practice in order to free up vets to focus on their jobs. In sum, a vet tech can do almost anything a vet can except diagnose illnesses, prescribe medications, and perform surgery. And it is most often the vet tech who knows how to provide the care that both pets and their owners need.

Becker considers veterinary nursing to be a critical part of any vet practice. He describes Michelle, the vet tech who provides nursing care at his North Idaho Animal Hospital, as much more than an assistant. Like all experienced vet techs, Michelle has an extensive body of knowledge that she brings to her work. For instance, she often notices symptoms and problems that the doctor has overlooked, and Becker highly values her diagnostic skills. He says, "Michelle and I typically discuss cases right in front of the pet owner. And far from making me, the veterinarian, look less smart and capable, her expertise complements my knowledge, experience and authority, and raises the pet owner's confidence in the quality of the care we are providing."[14]

A Typical Day on the Job

Jessica Krafthefer is a veterinary technician at Riverview Animal Hospital in Durango, Colorado. Her workdays are long and full, and she says about vet techs, "We wear a lot of hats."[15] Krafthefer begins her day working with dog patients who have slept overnight at the clinic. She takes them outside so that they can relieve themselves and then returns them to their kennels. Then she joins the whole hospital staff for morning rounds, during which each hospitalized animal is discussed. Plans are made for the day's appointments and surgeries. During the morning, Krafthefer assists with surgeries, monitoring anesthesia and the animal's vital signs, handing instruments to the vet, and lifting and moving an animal when the surgery is completed. She will check the animal frequently as it comes out of anesthesia, soothing it and ensuring that no problems arise.

After a quick lunch break, Krafthefer deals with the day's appointments. On one particular day, she takes X-rays of a dog who has swallowed a rock, cleans a wound on another dog, and then sits with a worried owner and takes a history of her dog's sickness. Krafthefer gently questions the owner about symptoms and behavior and then writes up notes about the case for the vet. The vet then sees the animal and in this case diagnoses it with gastroenteritis, which is inflammation of the stomach or intestines. Then it is up to Krafthefer to give the dog its medicine, fill the vet's prescription, and give the owner instructions for the animal's care.

Then, even though it is five o'clock, another vet in the hospital requires Krafthefer's help. He needs to use a scope to examine a dog's stomach, and the vet tech must feed the long tube down

Psychology for Pets

"Like veterinarians, technicians can also specialize in certain areas, such as radiology, dentistry, and anesthesiology. In my case, due to an abiding interest I had, I chose to specialize in behavior. I thought I could be of the most help to clients and their pets by helping them to overcome their behavioral problems as well as their medical ones. I have to say, the one thing I rarely experience in this field is boredom: You simply don't know what the day will bring!"

—Julie Shaw, registered veterinary technician

Julie Shaw, "Life as an 'Animal Psychiatric Nurse,'" Vetstreet, October 18, 2012. www. vetstreet.com.

the animal's throat while the vet uses the camera on the tube's end to diagnose the problem. The vet finds an obstruction in the stomach and must do immediate surgery. Once again, Krafthefer assists. Afterward, she checks on the animals that are staying overnight in the hospital. She then must enter computer records for all the patients that were seen that day. As frequently happens, Krafthefer ends up working late, but she does not complain. "It's hard work, but at the end of the day, when I go home exhausted, I still want to come back," she says. "Look at the amazing team I work with! You go home and think, 'Look what I accomplished today.' I wouldn't trade it for the world."[16]

How Do You Become a Vet Tech?

Typically, people attend two-year associate programs to become veterinary technicians. These programs are accredited by the American Veterinary Medical Association and are offered at community colleges, colleges and universities, and distance-learning, or online, programs. Some vet techs have attended four-year college programs and acquired a bachelor's degree in veterinary technology. A few become vet techs with on-the-job training, but for these people it can be difficult to acquire licensing and accreditation in other states.

Educational instruction for vet techs usually includes training in animal anatomy and physiology, animal behavior, pharmacology, radiology, surgery, and anesthesia. Most programs include practical course work in labs and internships in vet practices. After graduation, vet techs receive formal credentials by passing a state or federal examination. Each state regulates vet techs differently, so a vet tech may be credentialed as a licensed veterinary technician, a certified veterinary technician, or a registered veterinary technician. In most states vet techs must pass the Veterinary Technician National Examination to receive formal credentials, and the credentialing is transferrable to other states that use the same examination.

Working Conditions

In 2014, 91 percent of vet techs worked in veterinary services, including private clinics, hospitals, rescue organizations, zoos, and animal shelters. A vet tech's working conditions can be physically stressful and uncomfortable, even gross. Vet techs get urinated on or splashed with diarrhea or vomit. They must often deal with blood. They are expected to clean up and sterilize examining rooms after each appointment, no matter what bodily fluids have been left behind.

Vet techs suffer higher-than-average workplace injuries and illnesses because they commonly work with frightened or aggressive animals and sometimes infectious ones. When handling or restraining an animal, the vet tech can be bitten, scratched, or even kicked. In 2014, for instance, a vet tech at an animal emergency clinic in Hickory, North Carolina, was bitten by a dog brought in for treatment. The animal did not have the required vaccines and later tested positive for rabies—a deadly disease that can be transmitted to humans. The vet tech had to endure a series of shots to prevent the possibility of dying from the disease.

Such an occurrence is rare, but vet techs must always be aware of the dangers involved in their jobs.

The job can also be emotionally difficult. Vet techs often have to see abused or neglected animals or animals that are so old, sick, or injured that they have to be euthanized. They must support owners who are overwhelmed with grief for a dying companion. "The hardest part is probably when you put your all into helping a sick or injured animal, and in the end you can't," says vet tech Molly Bonacci. "You feel like you've failed that animal and his/her owner. Euthanasia is never easy either. Some people may say that it gets easier, but to me, it doesn't. I just have to try and think about something else in order to get through it."[17]

Personal Qualities

Dr. Joey Bryant says, "Veterinary technicians should be personable, hands-on animal lovers who have a genuine passion for improving animal welfare."[18] Along with caring about their patients, however, vet techs have to have good human communication skills, as well. They must not only impart accurate information to the veterinarian, but also explain medical diagnoses and recommendations to pet owners. Vet techs need to have the patience to deal with difficult animals and anxious humans and the stability to be emotionally calm in emergency situations. They also have to have the physical stamina and strength to stand for hours at a time (such as during surgeries) and to lift or restrain heavy animals when necessary.

Job Opportunities and Pay

Veterinary technicians are in high demand, and job opportunities are expected to continue to grow. The Bureau of Labor Statistics reports that the health of pets is of increasing importance to Americans, and pet parents' willingness to pay for medical treatments is growing, too. Because of this demand, veterinary practices are becoming more and more able and willing to hire vet techs who can provide quality nursing care.

Nevertheless, as one vet tech warns, "Do not go into veterinary technology for the money because there isn't any; we do this because we love veterinary medicine."[19] In 2014 veterinary technicians earned a median yearly income of $31,800. The lowest-paid salary was $21,390, while those making the highest salary earned $45,710.

Advancing Your Career

Vet techs have several opportunities to advance their careers. Experienced vet techs can become supervisors of veterinary support staff. In this capacity, the vet tech oversees the work of veterinary assistants (who have no formal training and provide basic care for animals) and newly credentialed vet techs. Vet techs also can continue their education and training and specialize in a specific area of animal care. Currently, there are eighteen different veterinary technician specialties, such as veterinary dental technician or veterinary technician specialist in anesthesia and analgesia. Vet techs who are certified in a specialty make more than the average salary. Also, many vet techs return to school and become veterinarians. Because of their certification and experience, vet techs often have an advantage in the veterinary medical school admissions process.

What Is the Future Outlook for Vet Techs?

Veterinary technology is a relatively new profession; the American Veterinary Medical Association only approved the designation in 1989. Since then vet techs have worked to establish their profession, define their skills, and develop national standards for certification and licensing. Today, as a result, educational opportunities have been dramatically expanded. Professional organizations such as the National Association of Veterinary Technicians in America have been established, veterinary technicians serve on the boards of veterinary associations such as the American Animal Hospital Association, and vet techs have two national journals devoted to their profession. On the national level, vet techs are discussing establishing national credentials for advanced levels of vet techs, like physician's assistants in human medicine. In the future vet techs can expect to see their nursing skills respected and utilized more and more in the modern world of animal care.

Find Out More

National Association of Veterinary Technicians in America (NAVTA)
PO Box 1227
Albert Lea, MN 56007
website: https://navta.site-ym.com

NAVTA is a professional organization open to vet techs, vet assistants, students, and educators. It maintains an extensive website and publishes a professional journal. Although much of its information is for members only, a lot of information is available to the general public about topics such as the role of vet techs, educational opportunities for vet techs, and the latest news from the veterinary world.

Today's Veterinary Technician
Eastern States Veterinary Association
5003 SW Forty-First Blvd.
Gainesville, FL 32608
website: http://todaysveterinarytechnician.com

Today's Veterinary Technician is an official journal of the North American Veterinary Community. The journal is written for vet techs, but its extensive collection of articles is available online for anyone to read. From dentistry for ferrets to puppy needs and behavior, there are topics for any interest.

VeterinarianEDU.org
website: www.veterinarianedu.org

This online resource was developed to describe veterinary careers. It details what a vet tech does, what the educational pathway is like, certification requirements, costs of an education, and future prospects for salary and jobs. It includes a list of information by state, as well as how to find a school and explanations of different veterinary careers.

Vet Tech Career Guide
website: www.veterinary-technician.net

This online resource is written and developed by two veterinary technicians with the goal of educating interested readers about the career. It includes advice and guidance about finding a certified educational program, studying for the national credentialing examination, determining if the career is right for you, and much more.

Pet Groomer

Pet groomers maintain the appearance and general health of companion animals—usually dogs, but sometimes cats as well. This includes bathing, brushing, trimming, clipping, and styling hair and fur. Groomers also cut nails, clean ears, express anal glands, de-mat fur, and offer salon-type skin treatments when necessary. A good groomer can make any pet look beautiful, please the most demanding pet owner, keep a pet comfortable and feeling its best, identify potential health problems (such as with skin or ears), and refer the owner for proper treatment. Most groomers say that their careers are enjoyable and rewarding and that they like going to work every day.

A Typical Day on the Job

Vickie Haywood has been a dog groomer for fifty-two years. She currently works in a shop with two other independent groomers. Although the groomers share the facilities and equipment, each sets her own schedule and decides which and how many animals to groom in a day. Groomers typically are able to schedule from four to eight clients a day, but on the typical day she describes, Haywood schedules only three dogs, with the first at 10:00 a.m. It is a large, calm dog that she bathes, blow-dries, and brushes. She trims the dog's coat, cleans its ears, and has no difficulty until it is time for a nail trim. Then there is a problem, as she explains: "All of a sudden it pushes a foot just as the nail clipper advances on the nail and OH OH, quicked [deeply cut] a nail, and now we have to deal with some blood. And remember to tell the owner we nicked a nail and what to do should it start to bleed again. SOME owners take this in stride, others, not so much."[20]

It takes Haywood about two hours to complete the grooming and send the dog home with its owner. She moves on to the client scheduled at noon . . . and encounters another problem. She gets the dog in the tub for its shampoo. Once the dog is clean and rinsed, Haywood goes to empty the dog's anal glands (sacs to the left and right of its anus that can get infected if not emptied), and the smelly fluid sprays all over the arm of her smock instead of into the tub. It's pretty disgusting. She tries to clean herself by washing her arm and sleeve in shampoo, but she knows she'll smell that bad odor for the rest of the day. Nevertheless, she successfully completes the grooming in about an hour and a half and sends the dog home with a satisfied owner.

Haywood has a break until the last scheduled appointment, so she runs a washer load of dirty towels and folds and puts away a previously cleaned and dried load of towels from the drier. She also vacuums the floor. Her last appointment is supposed to come at 2:00 p.m. but arrives late. It is a new client—a poodle—that has never been to this shop before. Poodles require extra time and attention because their coats need special clipping and cuts. This poodle does well for Haywood at first, but when it is time to blow-dry, the dog is terrified. Haywood holds the poodle on her lap to soothe it. She runs the drier on the lowest, quietest setting and finally finishes with the drying.

Next she has to clip the dog, but it is terrified of the clippers, too. She must clip its face, but the poodle fights every step of the way. Suddenly and without warning, the dog chomps down on Haywood's finger. As blood pours out of the wound, one of the other groomers brings her the first aid kit and helps her bandage the finger. It is not a serious injury, but it is right on the joint of the index finger she uses to grip her trimming scissors. She knows that the finger is going to be very sore when she is grooming the next day's clients. She finishes the clip anyway, and the dog looks beautiful, but Haywood is both tired and in pain.

Haywood's scheduled appointments are over for the day, and it is almost five o'clock, but she is far from ready to go home. The other two groomers have been seeing dogs all day, too, and all three must now clean and disinfect all the equipment in the shop, including the crates where dogs wait to be picked up by their owners, the tubs, and the floors. They wash a final load of towels and at last can close up shop.

Breaking Into the Business

No formal education is required to become a pet groomer. Many groomers get their start through an apprenticeship, which involves training with an experienced groomer. Such apprenticeships typically last about two months. This is how dog groomer Crystal Rolfe broke into the business. She started out as a bather in a small pet grooming shop. The owner of the shop began teaching Rolfe to do more. Rolfe says:

> When there was an opening in the grooming area she decided to start training me on the side. One or two days a week I would shadow her while she groomed a dog. Sometimes she would scissor one side and I'd scissor the other to match her. As my skills improved, I started to become even more excited about grooming. I never thought I could even cut hair let alone do it well.[21]

Rolfe became so committed to dog grooming that she began attending grooming seminars and then competing in grooming competitions. Ultimately, she sought and achieved certification from the International Society of Canine Cosmetologists.

A Great Profession

"It is a fun job, a rewarding job and—sometimes—even a dangerous job. If my 'customers' aren't happy, they don't just complain, they can bite or scratch! But I've mostly been able to successfully read my animal clients' state of mind, cater to their moods and complete their beautifying grooming to their satisfaction and mine. And, oh yes, to their owners' satisfaction, too. . . . Being a pet groomer is a truly rewarding career that gives back every day in doggie kisses and kitty licks. I don't know what could be a better way to spend the day at work!"

—Renee Mohan, Buffalo, NY, pet groomer

Renee Mohan, "Confessions of a Pet Groomer," AOL Finance, December 10, 2010. www.aol.com.

Schooling is the second main way to become a pet groomer. Licensed private grooming schools teach basic grooming, styling for different breeds, animal behavior, and general animal welfare. These programs can be two weeks to four months long. Upon graduation, most students receive a private certification or diploma. If a groomer wishes, he or she can apply to the National Dog Groomers Association of America to become a National Certified Master Groomer. The certification requires passing a written exam and a practical exam that demonstrates the groomer's skills. Certified master groomers command higher salaries and are often hired to groom for dog show competitions.

Working Conditions and Pay

Pet groomers may work for themselves, team up with other groomers to work in a private salon, work for a larger grooming business, be hired by a large chain pet store or veterinary service, or groom for an animal shelter. Wherever they work, the environment can be noisy, sometimes messy, and occasionally a little out of control, should a dog or cat freak out or act aggressively. Generally, an average dog grooming costs about sixty-five dollars, but the groomer does not get all of that if he or she works on salary or commission. Even those who work for themselves have overhead expenses, which include the cost of grooming tools and the insurance premiums necessary to cover the groomer should a dog be injured or escape and get lost while in the groomer's care. The average annual income for pet groomers is around $39,000, according to a 2016 survey.

Despite the financial stresses and the sometimes-demanding environment, pet grooming can be a lot of fun. "It's so cool to get to spend my whole day with pups," says groomer Jess Rona. "It's so rewarding to pamper the dogs *and* make my human clients happy: They drop off their stinky dog and at the end of the day, they get back a gorgeous, clean fluffball."[22]

Personal Qualities

A pet groomer must enjoy animals, but he or she must also be able to establish a good rapport and a trusting relationship with pet owners. Groomers need to be patient, calm, and compassionate

Advice for Prospective Groomers

"I strongly advise animal care students to visit a grooming parlour. Have a look [at] what's involved and see if pet grooming is suitable for you or not. Additionally, dog handling is very important as well. Not all dogs will stand still or sit still for you to groom. Being able to read the dog's body language is essential to the grooming process."

—Iris Chan, dog groomer in Australia

Quoted in Open Colleges, "Dog Grooming: Interview with Iris Chan, Doggy Stylist." www.opencolleges.edu.au.

in order to work with pets and people of all different personalities. They also must be willing to learn new skills throughout their careers. Pet grooming is a physically demanding job, so groomers must have strength (to lift and move large dogs), manual dexterity (to work with scissors, clippers, and other grooming tools), and stamina (to stand for long periods of time).

Sometimes, groomers also need emotional strength. At times, the groomer is the "first responder" who cleans and clips abused dogs that are confiscated in a puppy mill raid. The groomer's work is the first step in getting such a dog rescued and into an adoptive home, but seeing the horrible results of neglect is not easy. Also, when a longtime animal client sickens or dies, the groomer can experience real grief. Thankfully, most dogs that a groomer sees are loved and cherished family members, and groomers play a critical role in valuing each animal. As groomer Ellen Ehrlich explains, "When I attended grooming school I thought pet grooming was about a haircut and a bath; I could not have been more wrong. Grooming is all about love."[23]

What Is the Future Outlook for Pet Groomers?

Pet grooming is a growing business with a bright outlook. In the United States the amount of money spent on pets was more than $60 billion in 2015. Much of that money was spent on veterinary services, pet supplies, and food, but pet services (such as grooming and boarding) accounted for more than $5 billion of that amount. Pet parents love pampering their pets, and they are willing to pay the cost. Dog spas and salons are in demand and becoming common. Mobile pet grooming services, in which the groomer brings a van loaded with tools and tub to the pet's home, also are in high demand. In California, for instance, mobile groomers can start new businesses and quickly acquire so many customers that they have to turn down new clients. In that state a mobile groomer working full time can earn more than $78,000 per year. The Bureau of Labor Statistics predicts an 11 percent growth in demand for groomers throughout the country by 2024.

Find Out More

Groomer to Groomer
website: www.groomertogroomer.com

This online resource has news, videos, and articles written by and for groomers. Groomers educate, advise, inform, and encourage one another and describe their experiences on the job.

National Dog Groomers Association of America (NDGAA)
PO Box 101
Clark, PA 16113
website: www.nationaldoggroomers.com

The NDGAA emphasizes professional grooming standards and education. On its website, visitors can learn about the association's standards of care, sanitation, and safety recommendations.

PetGroomer.com
Find a Groomer
PO Box 2489
Yelm, WA 98597
website: http://petgroomer.com

PetGroomer.com is a website and online magazine. It offers a free monthly grooming magazine, an online community, a grooming school directory, and information about setting up a pet grooming business.

PetStylist.com
2702 Covington Dr.
Garland, TX 75040
website: www.petstylist.com

This is the site of the for-profit certification organization International Society of Canine Cosmetologists. It offers advanced education and certification examinations for dog groomers and a list of certified and approved schools.

Farrier

A Few Facts

Number of Jobs

About 25,000

Pay

Median income of $92,623 full time and $21,153 part time

Educational Requirements

None, but farrier trade school training strongly recommended

Personal Qualities

Ability to handle horses, physical strength, self-discipline

Work Settings

Outdoors on farms, ranches, stables, and racetracks; in show barns and blacksmith shops

Future Job Outlook

Solid job growth and increased demand expected from 2016 to 2026

Farriers are equine foot professionals. They shoe horses and adjust and shape the shoe to fit the horse. They trim and clip horse hooves to maintain good balance and prevent overgrown hooves. They also clean feet and evaluate horses' gaits and conformation in order to determine each horse's individual foot and limb needs.

You might think the need for farriers became obsolete one hundred years ago when the need for transportation horses disappeared as motor vehicles became common. However, 2 million people still own 9.2 million horses in the United States. When those animals need foot care, their owners call a farrier, because few owners know how to care for a horse's feet themselves. Horse hooves need routine trimming, and horseshoes regularly need to be replaced when the horse pulls them off, which happens if they get stuck in mud or if one foot steps on the shoe of another. Farriers work with horses used for racing, showing, recreation, breeding, and farmwork. Just in routine hoof care alone, a full-time farrier performs an average of nineteen hundred trimmings a year.

A Typical Day on the Job

More than 90 percent of farriers are self-employed. This means they arrange their own schedules and travel from appointment to appointment in their trucks or vans while carrying the tools they need, which includes portable anvils, rasps, and nippers for shaping hoofs. Although many farriers say there is no such thing as a typical day, farrier Leigh Ballard describes a day that is representative of his work. He starts out early so as to get to his first appointment at 5:30 a.m. At this barn, two horses are scheduled for shoeing. Usually, farriers do not fashion horseshoes themselves. They carry a variety of ready-made shoes that they can adjust and fit to an individual horse's feet.

After shoeing the horses, Ballard has to drive about an hour to get to the next appointment. He arrives at a barn of show horses that are performing that weekend. He checks, cleans, and trims each horse's hooves. Horse hooves are always growing, just like toenails and fingernails. Therefore, horses typically need their hooves trimmed every six to eight weeks. Next Ballard moves on to a farm where a couple of horses are kept for recreation. These horses do not get their hooves trimmed often enough, so Ballard spends extra time with them. During this visit, he also takes an emergency phone call from a horse owner who thinks her horse has an abscess (a pus-filled swelling) on one foot. Ballard agrees to come by her farm first thing the next morning.

Ballard's afternoon and evening are devoted to more hoof care and trimmings at different farms. He says, "This is a typical day for a successful full-time farrier—often more than eight hours long, many miles, an expensive tank of fuel, several horses, and gallons of water. It's back-breaking work, and goes from spring to fall, with some respite in winter."[24]

Not all farriers work such long hours, since each is able to set his or her own working hours. Tom Clothier, for example, is a farrier in the United Kingdom. He usually works eight-hour days and takes time off every weekend. Still, he has about one hundred regular clients who schedule him to provide hoof care for their horses. Clothier holds a certificate in forging and is skilled in providing the right shoes for each individual horse. An estimated 80 percent of lameness in horses is caused by incorrect shoeing that throws the horse off balance. One particular kind of lameness, called laminitis, can be treated and corrected with proper shoeing. Clothier is particularly happy when he can make a lame horse sound (free of injury and in good condition). He says, "My favourite part of the job is dealing with a poorly horse that has say laminitis, through shoeing methods we can literally save horses lives or [bring] a lame horse through to soundness with shoes."[25]

How Do You Become a Farrier?

Although no formal training or education is required, most prospective farriers attend farrier or horseshoeing school and then seek certification. Without these formal credentials, it is extremely difficult to break into the business and build up a base of clients who will respect and trust you. In the United States there are about fifty public and private horseshoeing schools. A good school typically offers a minimum of two months' instruction and about 320 hours of education. Some schools, especially ones where you can train to become a master farrier and learn the blacksmithing skills to make shoes from scratch, can take two to four years to complete. In a basic school, however, students get a good foundation in hoof trimming, horseshoeing, and horse anatomy and physiology. They

Having What It Takes

"The job requires much more than putting shoes on a horse. You need knowledge of the anatomy of a horse, what kind of work they're doing, their conformation, and any existing and old injuries. You need to be pretty fit, with a strong back and core to do the work of shoeing horses, and for that reason it's still a job dominated by men. But I'm strong."

—Elli Nash, female farrier

Quoted in George Farrell, "What's Up: A Farrier's Future," Highlander Online, January 2, 2015. http:// highlanderonline.cmshelplive.net.

learn to recognize health problems and work with veterinarians to evaluate lameness, and they also acquire skills in general horsemanship. Students receive academic instruction as well as get the chance to experience hands-on learning. Under the supervision of instructors, students clean feet, trim hooves, and shoe horses. Students and instructors often go out in the local community and service horses at a reduced cost so the students can gain experience.

After they finish school, most farriers choose to get certified with a professional organization, such as the American Farrier's Association. At that point, many farriers seek to work with an established farrier as an apprentice to gain even more experience before striking out on their own.

Starting a Business

Establishing yourself as a farrier is mostly a word-of-mouth process—many get clients via recommendations and the personal contacts made during apprenticeships with other farriers or in the community. "It's kind of slow-building," says farrier Brian Crandall of getting started. "It's getting recommendations from veterinarians, kind of who you know and just being out there."[26]

As with any small business, farriers have some start-up costs. These include the extensive variety of tools needed for the trade, as well as a vehicle to carry all the equipment. Most find that insurance is a necessity, too, to protect themselves if they are injured on the job and can't work or if a horse under their care is injured. To be successful, a farrier needs to be self-disciplined and motivated, keep good records, and be patient enough to slowly build up the business. Farrier John Suttle says that a farrier must be a good manager and planner when it comes to schedules and making appointments. "Planning makes a huge difference in how smoothly your business runs," he says. "This is your business, take charge and make it what you want and need it to be."[27]

Finally, a farrier needs to maintain his or her physical health if the business is to be a success. According to the website Farrier

Guide, four hours of farrier work is as physically demanding as eight hours of construction work. A farrier has to be like an athlete and work to keep in strong, flexible condition.

Working Conditions

Farriers spend about 75 percent of their time bent over at the waist and lifting and holding a horse's lower limb. Fifteen consecutive minutes of this posture and activity is physically demanding, especially when you consider that a horse can weigh 1,200 pounds (544 kg) and may not want to cooperate. Farriers need strong backs, legs, and wrists. Many report finishing a workweek with sore backs and muscles.

Other injuries are a risk of the trade, too. Farriers often need to work with skittish, nervous, or aggressive horses and must learn how to soothe the animals. Even the most experienced farriers run the risk of being kicked, bitten, knocked down, or slammed into a stable wall. Sometimes they are sprayed with manure from one end of the horse or saliva mixed with hay from the other.

The general environment of a working farrier is usually dusty, dirty, noisy, and often hot. Most farriers carry extra shirts and towels with them so that they can change clothes when they get too sweaty or dirty. One farrier says that it is not unusual to drink about 2 gallons (7.6 L) of water in a day.

Personal Qualities

A farrier has to enjoy and understand horses, but he or she must also like and communicate well with people, since they are the ones doing the hiring. Otherwise, says Mark Plumlee, farrier and owner of the Mission Farrier School, it is fairly simple to be successful. "I tell my students, if you are a good listener, you will learn," he says. "After that, if you return phone calls and show up on time, you'll have all the business you want." He also encourages his students to be clean, professional, and polite. "Bad language just shows you are too ignorant to have a better vocabulary, and leaving nails on the ground, it's just not professional. If you are lazy natured or complacent, don't bother. Do something else."[28]

What Is the Future Outlook for Farriers?

Skillful, experienced, trustworthy farriers are in high demand. The American Farrier's Association predicts increasing opportunities for farriers in the future as more and more people own horses and seek hoof care services. Although the trade remains dominated by men, some 10 percent of farriers are women, and with education and experience, they are entering the profession and thriving in increasing numbers.

Find Out More

American Association of Professional Farriers (AAPF)
PO Box 223
West Palm Beach, FL 33422
website: http://professionalfarriers.com

The AAPF is a trade organization for professional farriers. Its mission is to further the knowledge of its members, as well as provide accreditation, support, and communication within the profession. At its website, people can explore recommended farrier schools and mentoring programs or search for a farrier in their area.

American Farrier's Association (AFA)
AFA Headquarters
4059 Iron Works Pkwy., Suite #1
Lexington, KY 40511
website: https://americanfarriers.org

The AFA is the oldest professional organization for farriers in the United States. It provides certification examinations for its members and is recognized throughout the world for its competency standards. Visitors to the website can learn about farrier schools and how to locate a farrier, as well as read articles written for farriers in the association's newsletters.

Farrier Guide
website: www.thefarrierguide.com

This online resource offers extensive information about the farrier trade. Topics include a description of the farrier's work, educational opportunities, how to set up a business, a discussion of farrier supplies, and much more.

Texas Horseshoeing School
PO Box 188
Scurry, TX 75158
website: www.texashorseshoeingschool.com

The Texas Horseshoeing School is a good example of a quality farrier school that makes it easy for a student to gain necessary skills and be certified by a professional association. At the school's website, prospective students can learn about the courses offered, the kind of instruction available, and the experience of attending farrier school.

Fish and Game Warden

Fish and game wardens are also known as wildlife officers, conservation officers, or just game wardens. They are first and foremost law enforcement professionals. They work for state, local, and federal governments to protect and manage wildlife. Their job is to enforce federal and state laws, investigate reports of crop or property damage caused by wildlife, and collect biological data to determine the health of wildlife populations. Fish and game wardens combine the job of managing wildlife and habitats with enforcing the law. They know that hunting and fishing regulations are a critical way to protect wildlife populations. Every warden is a certified peace officer as well as a conservation expert.

Job duties vary by state and region, but in general, wardens patrol outdoor areas in the woods, along the ocean shore, by rivers, in deserts, in the mountains, and even in some city areas. They may need to patrol their assigned areas on foot, on horseback, in all-terrain vehicles or other vehicles, or from airplanes and boats. They are always on the lookout for poachers, illegal trappers, polluters, and other lawbreakers. They ensure that fishing and hunting licenses are current and that hunters or fishers are abiding by the law (such as respecting hunting boundaries and catch limits). They also may help biologists and conservationists identify wildlife or environmental problems and conduct scientific research of wildlife in a specific area. If you are interested in a career with diverse responsibilities in the great outdoors, you might consider becoming a fish and game warden.

A Typical Day on the Job

Michael Boone is one of five hundred game wardens who work for the Texas Parks and Wildlife Department. He describes a quiet but typical day on his job one Saturday. He starts out in his state-issued truck at eight o'clock in the morning, checking the camps of some hunting clubs in his assigned area. He talks with the hunters he meets, asks questions about how hunting is going and if they have seen or heard anything unusual, and just generally makes it obvious that he is around and on the job. Boone explains that building relationships is important because he can get information and tips from friendly citizens. He says:

> In the past, particularly in East Texas, game wardens were not welcomed with open arms into some of these hunting clubs, some of these ranches. Over the years, with a little education, building up a rapport around your community, getting to know some of these guys, they understand we're only out there trying to help them, help them maintain control over their hunting clubs, their ranches, their private properties.[29]

Boone is looking for people who have shot more game than their licenses allow. He stops and checks a couple of hunters and their licenses as he drives along the country dirt roads, but everything is routine and legitimate. By noon, he is finished with his morning duties and can go home. He has a break until he begins his evening patrol at five o'clock. Since it is illegal to hunt at night,

A game warden confiscates a reticulated python from an individual who was unlicensed to keep it. Fish and game wardens are law enforcement officers whose job is to protect and manage wildlife populations.

it is important that he be a visible presence and seek out any illegal activity during this time.

First Boone stops at a marsh where he knows duck hunters often lie in wait; some may try to break the rules by shooting after the sun goes down. He sits still in his truck until the sun has set, waiting to be sure that he hears no shots. Then he moves on to two different deer hunting camps, showing up unannounced so that all the hunters know he is around and on the job. All is quiet at both camps, so at about seven o'clock the warden drives to an old roadway that he knows illegal hunters have used in the past. He turns off his headlights and sits in the dark to be sure no one shows up. Sometimes, if Boone has gotten a tip from one of the hunters, he will go back to such a spot over and over for weeks to finally catch an illegal hunter. On this night, however, no shots ring out. By nine o'clock, Boone has finished his workday and can go home.

Not all of a game warden's days are as calm as this one. For instance, a game warden identified as Alice once received a report of a trespasser on a hunting camp's property while she was on night patrol. As she pulled into the campground, she spotted a car with its headlights on and shining into the woods. This is called spotlighting—a hunting technique that makes animals freeze blindly and is illegal. No one was in or near the car, but Alice quietly waited, watching the edge of the woods. Soon she saw the form of a man carrying a heavy load come out of the woods. She sprang into action, pulling out her firearm and calling firmly, "County Game Warden, drop what you're carrying and put your hands over your head."[30] The man was a poacher, illegally hunting a deer at night. Alice successfully arrested him and had him in jail within the hour.

"Like any other law enforcement officer, conservation officers may have to deal with dangerous situations," says Nebraska conservation officer Dina Hopper Lincon. She tells an even scarier story. "One night I had to chase a drunk driver who nearly ran over several people in their campground. He jumped in the lake and tried to swim away from me, so I chased him down in the boat and caught him. It turns out he was wanted for a number of assault charges."[31] Lincon's arrest of a dangerous criminal is a reminder that wardens are law enforcement officers first.

How Do You Become a Fish and Game Warden?

The federal government and many states require that fish and game wardens have a bachelor's degree. Some states accept a two-year associate's degree with related experience. Typical college majors for those wishing to become game wardens include wildlife biology, ecology, environmental science, and law enforcement. Education, however, is just the first step toward a career. To get hired at the state or federal level, applicants must be at least twenty-one years old, hold a valid driver's license, and be a US citizen or legal resident. They cannot have any felony convictions at all or any misdemeanor convictions for domestic violence. All states and the federal government require that prospective employees pass psychological, physical, and medical fitness testing.

After getting hired, wardens must successfully complete a training academy program. At the federal level, trainees do twenty weeks of basic training at the Federal Law Enforcement Training Center in Glynco, Georgia. Trainees receive firearms and law enforcement instruction as well as instruction in wildlife laws and enforcement. Following this period new game wardens spend forty-four weeks receiving field training under game wardens at their assigned duty stations.

State training requirements vary, but all require a period of basic law enforcement, firearms, and wildlife management schooling. They also require probationary or field training that must be completed before the new game warden can work independently.

Working Conditions

Fish and game wardens spend most of their days in the field, patrolling an assigned area, interacting with the public, and often coordinating their activities with sheriff's departments and police. They are uniformed officers who usually patrol alone and always carry a firearm. They are out in all kinds of weather conditions and at all times of the day and night. Many wardens work long overtime hours and on holidays and weekends. Sometimes, especially in rural areas, they are on call twenty-four hours a day.

Although most daily activities are routine, wardens sometimes face hazardous conditions and dangerous situations. They may patrol icy, snowy, or flooded roads; brave a blizzard to rescue

Quick Thinking in a Dangerous Situation

"I got a call that people were shocking fish one night [illegally using electrical power in water to kill fish]. I put in my boat. . . . I eased up on them, and when I got real close, I turned my spotlight on them and shouted, 'Game warden!'

They took off.

I was chasing them down the river in complete darkness. . . . The guy running the motor, well, I knew who he was, and he had a reputation for carrying a pistol in his pocket. . . . I was like, 'I've got to put a stop to this.' So I pulled my pistol out and shot his motor. Well, that ended that chase."

—Bret Staggs, retired Arkansas game warden

Quoted in Arkansas Life, "Telling Tails," November 2014. http://arkansaslife.com.

an injured hunter or a lost child; or cope with 100-degree (38°C) weather as they slog through a swamp to investigate suspicious activity. Wardens also occasionally have to deal with injured or aggressive wildlife that bite, scratch, or kick. Sometimes these animals need to be rescued, but at other times they need to be humanely euthanized.

Many of the dangers that wardens deal with, however, come from people. Almost all the people the warden comes in contact with on patrol are armed, perhaps with knives, guns, or other weapons. Sometimes these people are belligerent or hostile; sometimes they are drunk or high on drugs; sometimes they are lawbreakers. Always, the game warden must be able to cope with these situations with good judgment, quick thinking, and decisive action.

Personal Qualities

Game wardens love the outdoors, nature, and animals, and they are passionate about protecting wildlife. However, they must also

The Importance of Diplomacy

"As law enforcement officers, game wardens are tasked with enforcing all Nevada state laws and, many times, we are doing so when those we come in contact with have weapons on them. That's always a challenge that we try to keep in mind and approach differently than others in our field. . . . We try to relate to people and portray ourselves, as an agency, in a positive light. We are out there for the good of everyone."

—Buck Tingle, Nevada game warden

Quoted in Heidi Bethel, "Nature's Calling," *Edible Reno-Tahoe Magazine*, 2014. www.ediblerenotahoe.com.

be skilled at communicating and interacting with people. "This is not a job for someone who doesn't like dealing with people," says Shane Reno, a game warden in Montana. "Whether we're answering questions about state park camping fees or untangling fish hooks for a bunch of third-graders, the essence of being a warden is being able to work with people."[32]

At the same time, game wardens are courageous and do not mind taking risks. Dina Hopper Lincon explains that she finds the challenges of her job exciting. She says, for example, "I think most conservation officers enjoy catching spotlighters. It is some of the most adrenaline rushing work we do."[33] Game wardens have to be responsible, conduct themselves with integrity, and work independently under stressful conditions—but that does not mean that they can't enjoy their work. Says Missouri game warden George Allerby, "I get to work outdoors, meet new people and catch bad guys. On top of that, they pay me for it!"[34]

What Is the Future Outlook for Fish and Game Wardens?

The number of fish and game wardens hired by state and federal governments tends to remain stable over time. Most new hires are to replace older wardens who are retiring. The number of projected job openings between 2014 and 2024 is expected to be about two thousand.

Find Out More

GameWardenEDU.org
website: www.gamewardenedu.org

This private online resource can be used as a guide by anyone interested in becoming a fish and game warden. It provides state and federal requirements, job descriptions, salary information, and a guide to finding a school with a degree program suited to an individual's interests.

Game Warden.org
website: www.gamewarden.org

This website offers a comprehensive resource for anyone interesting in learning about a career as a game warden. It includes a state-by-state listing of eligibility requirements, descriptions of academic majors related to the profession, and many articles about what it is like to be a game warden.

US Fish & Wildlife Service
1849 C St. NW
Washington, DC 20240
website: www.fws.gov

Federal game wardens typically work in the law enforcement arm of the US Fish & Wildlife Service. At the official government website for the service, people can learn about the extensive work for nature preservation and conservation done by this bureau of the US Department of the Interior.

Primatologist

Primatology is the scientific study of nonhuman primates, such as gorillas, monkeys, chimpanzees, and lemurs. It is a varied discipline with a wide range of different specialties and interests. In general, however, primatologists are scientists who study and gather data on primates, either in academia and laboratory research or in the field.

Perhaps the world's most famous primatologist is Jane Goodall. She was a trailblazer in primatology during the 1960s, studying chimpanzees in their natural habitat and establishing standards of observation that are still accepted today. Goodall made discoveries about chimp behavior and culture that amazed the scientific community. She energized and inspired generations of scientists and young people who wanted to learn about the secret lives of all kinds of animals. Even now she continues to work to persuade people to cherish and protect primate species. Today extending our knowledge of primates and preserving them in their natural environment is the mission of scientists with diverse academic backgrounds such as biology, zoology, psychology, anthropology, and veterinary sciences. However, all identify themselves as primatologists, and all have a passion for understanding these complex, fascinating creatures.

A Typical Day on the Job

Colin Chapman is a primatologist and professor at McGill University in Canada. He combines both academic work and fieldwork in his career. His interest is in how plants in the environment affect primate behavior and populations and, conversely, how primates affect the plants in their ecosystems. His typical days vary immensely, depending on which role he is playing. During his academic time at the university, he works behind a desk, analyzing research data, writing papers, and interacting with peers and students. In the field, however, his typical day is far from staid and ordinary. He works in his research station in Kibale National Park in Uganda.

At the research station, Chapman gets up by about five o'clock in the morning to get his day scheduled and have breakfast. By seven thirty he meets with his two teams of Ugandan field assistants. They are all long-term, knowledgeable observers in the field. On this day they are continuing their research on red colobus monkeys. Chapman assigns one team to go out into a specific large area to collect different primate foods and to count the number of food-bearing trees in the vicinity. He and the other team search out and observe the red colobus group that has become habituated to (used to) their presence. Everyone takes extensive notes of the behavior they see in the monkeys throughout the day. Chapman says, "I can easily say that my favorite part of my job is to watch monkeys, see what they are doing, and speculate on why. I feel honored and amazed that I am actually paid to do this."[35]

Chapman may also spend part of his day in the field doing a census. This means he collects data about the plant species in particular areas of the park and counts the number of primate communities that he finds in the different areas. For instance, he may observe whether baboons are common in one kind of habitat or which specific areas support the most blue monkey groups. Chapman is passionate about conservation, understanding how to keep primate populations healthy, and educating local populations to appreciate and protect the primates in the park.

Following the Gorillas

Bethan J. Morgan also cares about and studies primate populations in their natural habitats. She earned her doctorate from the University of Cambridge, studying elephants, gorillas, and chimpanzees. Today she is particularly interested in conservation efforts with endangered primates, such as some types of gorillas and the drills of Cameroon. She has spent years living and working in Central Africa as a primatologist and describes some of what she encounters in a typical day in Ebo National Park in Cameroon.

Her research station is deep in the wilderness, about an eight-hour walk from the nearest village. Conditions are basic and primitive, with oil lamps for light and open fires for cooking. Her research team uses tents and tarps for shelter. Morgan explains, "Overall, the prospective primatologist shouldn't expect luxury—the goal of most research stations is to limit the amount of time needed to fulfill the most basic of human needs so that time for data collection can be maximized."[36]

Like Chapman when he is in Uganda, Morgan gets up around 5:30 a.m. to spend the day in the field, starting at sunrise. She and her local team head off into the forest, equipped with tools of the trade such as notebooks and pencils, voice recorders,

Gaining Chimpanzees' Trust

"I always wore clothes of the same colour. I never tried to get too close too quickly and for a long time I didn't even try to follow them. I didn't make any sudden movements. I didn't talk loudly. I was just there. I didn't interfere with them. I was just part of the landscape."

—Jane Goodall, primatologist

Quoted in *Focus*, "Interview with Primatologist Jane Goodall," Egon Zehnder, 2017. www.egonzehnder .com.

Global Positioning System devices, compasses, cameras, collection bags, and supplies like lunch. On this day, she and her team follow a group of unhabituated gorillas. Unhabituated gorillas are not used to people and run away from them. The team members rarely get a glimpse of their subjects. Instead, they study the animals indirectly. For instance, they observe and collect droppings that tell them the size of the animal and what it has eaten. They also collect data about the gorilla sleeping nests, which are built anew in trees every night. By following the trail the gorillas leave each day, the researchers learn the size of the group, its territorial boundaries, and more. They even collect DNA from hair and droppings. Morgan prefers this indirect observational approach at times because she worries about gorillas losing their fear of humans and becoming vulnerable to poaching.

The team returns to camp by nightfall, cooks a simple dinner over an open fire, socializes a little while, reviews and fleshes out data notes, and turns in early so as to be ready to repeat the whole process the next day. Morgan says life in the field is intense but brings her a lot of joy.

How Do You Become a Primatologist?

Primatologists have a wide variety of educational backgrounds, but most need a minimum of a four-year college degree. In college, students take many science-oriented courses, such as biology, evolutionary biology, genetics, anthropology, zoology, psychology, ecology, and veterinary medicine. In addition, courses in statistics and computer science are often a necessity. There are no undergraduate majors in primatology, so students generally tailor their courses to their particular interests. For example, students interested in animal behavior might major in psychology, while those interested in caring for captive primates in zoos might concentrate on veterinary medicine.

After graduation, some students get experience working with primates through internships and volunteer positions, perhaps at zoos or even in the field. In many cases interns and volunteers

Happiness and Challenges in the Field

"Finding the owl monkeys early at dawn; spotting their silhouettes against the sky at the break of dawn fascinates me today like it did back in 1996, when I saw them for the first time. And a full moon night—what an incredible experience to be in the forest with a full moon. . . . The most challenging experience was capturing our first owl monkey to fit it [with] a radio collar. We worked and planned and prepared for that day for months, and it took months to succeed."

—Eduardo Fernandez-Duque, Argentine primatologist

Quoted in *National Geographic*, "Eduardo Fernandez-Duque: Primatologist." www .nationalgeographic.com.

have to cover their own expenses, and such positions can be hard to come by. However, those who succeed say the experience is extremely valuable and satisfying.

Postgraduate education in a doctoral primatology program, medical school, or veterinary school is generally required for anyone who wants to advance in the field of primatology, whether as a lab researcher, in academia as a professor, or in the field. Primatology doctoral programs usually take about six years to complete.

Working Conditions

As Chapman and Morgan point out, primatologists who work in the field face difficult conditions. "You'll not only have to do without modern medical facilities, but also without electricity, running water, TV, and shopping as you know it," says primatologist Kevin Hunt. "You can pretty much count on getting some kind of tropical disease, and you'll be very lucky if you don't get malaria."[37] Hunt also says that field observation isn't always as romantic as it seems. There is a lot of day-to-day drudgery and hard work, whether spending hours trying to make contact with elusive primates or writing up reports. Researchers often have to deal with sometimes-distressing cultural diversity, human poverty and disease, and bad food, too.

Primatologist Kathryn Shutt echoes Hunt's warnings about working conditions from her experiences doing fieldwork in Liberia. She says that while the camps may be remote, the field team finds it hard to get any privacy, especially when they need to bathe in a stream or use the bathroom in the same hole dug in the ground. There are also health risks. "In most primate range places there is a risk of tropical diseases and I've had just about everything," she says. "You're out there thinking, in some ways it's so great to be so at one with nature, but you actually wake up dreading that you're going to be run down by an elephant or bitten by a snake."[38]

Personal Qualities

Primatologists have strong scientific interests. They are also extremely patient and attentive to detail. Many say that they also have to be willing to make sacrifices, whether in the area of physical comfort, facing risks and challenges, living in unfamiliar environments, or spending extensive periods of time separated from family and friends. They have to have good people and communication skills, be good team players, and be sensitive to the needs of local cultures. Above all, primatologists are passionate about studying and protecting primates and fascinated by life in a wild ecosystem.

What Is the Future Outlook for Primatologists?

Primatology is a highly competitive field in which there are more applicants than there are jobs available. That is why acquiring a doctorate is almost a necessity. Much of the problem is that the work of primatology is mostly dependent on government funding, and the money for field and research projects depends on government interest and the availability of finances. However, human populations around the world are becoming more and more concerned about environmental issues and conservation efforts, and scientists have hope that there will be increased funding for these kinds of projects in the future.

Although job demand is expected to grow about 5 percent over the next ten years, it takes hard work to establish a career, especially in fieldwork. Nevertheless, it is achievable. "You have to be enormously dedicated," says Hunt. "Almost all of the primatologists I know simply refused to be told no, and kept trying until they finally got into the field. Most people will give up, but if you're willing to make the sacrifices and persevere, you WILL eventually succeed."[39]

Find Out More

American Society of Primatologists
website: www.asp.org

This nonprofit organization of primatologist members promotes the exchange of information among members and education for all who are interested in nonhuman primates. The society publishes the *American Journal of Primatology*, devoted to the latest research findings in the field. Visitors to the website can read abstracts of the journal articles and some full articles. In addition, click the Research link to learn about what research with primates entails.

Jane Goodall Institute—USA Headquarters
1595 Spring Hill Rd., Suite 550
Vienna, VA 22182
website: www.janegoodall.org

Established by Jane Goodall, the institute is devoted to conserving great apes and educating humanity about the wonders and value of the natural world. The website is full of information about Goodall's work, the institute's story, chimpanzees, how people can volunteer or acquire primatology experience and education, and how to help save primates everywhere.

Primate Education Network (PEN)

c/o Social Good Fund
PO Box 5473
Richmond, CA 94801
website: www.primateeducationnetwork.org

PEN is a global community of educators dedicated to advancing conservation education programs about primates. Visitors to the PEN website can listen to stories from members about their education efforts in various parts of the world and how their efforts impact the health of local primate populations.

Wisconsin National Primate Research Center (WNPRC)

Office of the Vice Chancellor for Research and Graduate Education, University of Wisconsin
333 Bascom Hall
500 Lincoln Dr.
Madison, WI 53706
website: www.primate.wisc.edu

At the WNPRC website, visitors can access information about primate research, educational opportunities, and primatology discoveries. Locate the link for Primate Info Net for an extensive library of information about what primatologists do and how to explore career options in primatology. There is even a section on primate jobs currently available for people seeking volunteer opportunities and internships.

Entomologist

Some people love and are fascinated by bugs. For them, entomology—the study of insects and related arthropods (such as spiders)—is the perfect career choice. In general, entomologists study insects in reference to their relationship to people, other animals, and the environment. Most entomologists concentrate on a particular kind of insect, but there are many different specialty areas, and entomologists may do many different things. Agricultural entomologists, for example, study how to protect crops from insect pests while not harming beneficial insects. Veterinary and medical entomologists study the diseases that insects transmit to animals and people, respectively, and how to protect against the insects or prevent infestations. Forensic entomologists help homicide investigators solve murders by studying the insects associated with dead bodies; it is possible to determine the time of death and the location of a murder based on the insects. Taxonomic entomologists search for previously unknown and unidentified insects in the wild, study how the insects evolved, and determine what role they play in ecological systems. (*Taxonomic* refers to how creatures are classified.)

Entomologists may work in academia, for government agencies, with private corporations, in medicine, at zoos, in museums, or with environmental organizations. No matter where they work or in which specialty area, they study and understand classification systems and species identification, life cycles, behavior, physiology, and population distributions of insects. If you want to know anything about a bug's life, ask an entomologist!

A Typical Day on the Job

Because entomologists can have such diverse careers, there is no one kind of typical day that represents the profession. But Eric R. Eaton describes a typical day for him doing research in the field and then in the lab. At the time, he was engaged in a large project concerned with studying the health of forested watersheds. These ecosystems are common in the northeastern United States, but they are important and complex habitats nonetheless. Many different scientists were involved in the project, but since insects are a critical part of every ecosystem, Eaton was the entomologist of the group. The previous week he had set pitfall traps in a series of dry streambeds. The plastic traps are buried in the ground and set so that the opening lies flush with the surface, and any insects that come along fall into the lip of the trap and cannot escape.

Eaton collects all the traps, marks where they were set, and writes down the date the insects were collected. He then returns the traps to his lab. There he preserves the contents of the trap with alcohol. Then he picks out all the insects, spiders, and other creatures and puts each one into a separate glass vial. He labels the vial with the specimen's name (type of beetle, for instance) and its collection location. He records that data on a master sheet that will contain all the information from that day's collection results. Next Eaton turns to his microscope to identify whatever specimens in the trap are too small to see with the naked eye. Usually he has no trouble assigning correct scientific names to those specimens, too. These results are recorded. All of the data

accumulated is combined with data from previous weeks and future weeks to slowly build up a database of insect life in the ecosystem. It is work that can continue for months or years.

Eaton goes out into the field to collect his specimens, but not all entomologists work in the field. For example, British entomologist Nina Stanczyk does medical research on mosquito populations that are raised in cages in her laboratory. She is studying mosquitos because in many parts of the world they are infected with malaria that they pass on to people when they bite. Stanczyk has a theory about how smell can be used to prevent mosquito bites and malaria. "Mosquitoes use our odor to track us down from a distance and bite us," she explains. "If we can isolate the chemicals in our smell that they find attractive, we may be able to make lures and traps for monitoring the population. If we isolate chemicals they find repellent, we can look at developing new repellents for people to use as personal protection."[40] She theorizes that malarial mosquitos might be attracted to different chemical smells than uninfected mosquitos.

On a typical day the first thing Stanczyk does is check on her mosquitos and collect a sample of females for experiments. (Only female mosquitos bite.) Under extremely controlled safety conditions, she infects half the mosquitos with the malaria parasite (also grown in the lab under isolated, containment conditions). Then she begins the day's experiments. "I carry out behavioral experiments to compare the infected and uninfected mosquitoes," she says. "These could be flying mosquitoes down a wind tunnel to see which smell they prefer—which has to be done in the dark, as these are night feeders—or putting a sock on a cage (mosquitoes love human foot odor) to see how many mosquitoes try to bite it." Stanczyk's ultimate goal is to develop a way to help humanity with her work. She adds, "Once we know more about the response of infected mosquitoes to specific chemicals, we hope to develop an odor for traps that will target mosquitoes carrying the malaria parasites. This will prevent them being able to bite people and transmit the disease."[41] Since about 1 million people around the world die of malaria every year, Stanczyk's research could greatly benefit humanity in the future.

How Do You Become an Entomologist?

The minimum educational level needed for a job in entomology is a four-year college degree. Few universities offer an undergraduate entomology degree, so students typically major in biology, zoology, ecology, or a related scientific field and take any available courses in insects and entomology. With a bachelor's degree, an individual might be able to get a job as a laboratory assistant or help survey a forest's insect population. Usually, however, an entomologist needs a postgraduate degree to work. In graduate school students can specialize in entomology. With a master's degree entomologists may become lab assistants or junior researchers, or they may find work in pest control or identifying insects for a private environmental consulting business.

At the doctoral level entomologists can conduct research and teach in universities. Most entomologists need doctorates. This means another two or three years of education after the master's degree in which you specialize in insects and perhaps concentrate on a specific area, such as insect pathology, pest management, or evolutionary biology.

Certification

On a voluntary basis, you can become a Board Certified Entomologist (BCE) by meeting qualifications set by the Entomological Society of America. The society administers a general exam plus specialized ones (such as in plant-related or medical entomology). Applicants must pass the general exam and at least one of the specialized exams. To be eligible to take the exams, entomologists with a bachelor's degree must have three years of work experience. Those with master's degrees must have two years of experience, while those with doctorates need one year of experience. In order to keep the BCE credential in good standing, every certified entomologist is required to complete a set amount of continuing education or professional participation (such as attending conferences) hours every three years. BCEs are most valued by employers and have the most opportunities to advance in the profession.

Working Conditions

Many entomologists with doctorates are university or college faculty members, although others work in offices and laboratories, both public and private. Most are also involved in fieldwork of some kind. Fieldwork can be strenuous and physically demanding. Entomologists may travel to forests, jungles, mountains, savannas, and even oceans to study the insects of different ecosystems. They may live in primitive camping conditions and be out in the field in all kinds of weather. They may also face dangers from wildlife and the insects they study. George McGavin is one entomologist who has traveled the world studying insects. "You need to be careful especially in jungles," he says. "I was once attacked by a

The Joy of Insects

"I have field-collected insect colonies and specimens in countries such as Trinidad, New Guinea, and Malaysia. I'll never forget the excitement of my first major collection expedition to Costa Rica. We arrived at the field station late at night and walked the paths with flashlights. We were surrounded by a symphony of sound. It was so exciting and every leaf held another insect—each one unique and mysterious. I had read about the biodiversity in tropical rain forests, but experiencing it firsthand was incredible."

—Leslie Saul Gershenz, conservation entomologist

Quoted in Entomological Society of America, "Leslie Saul Gershenz, Conservation Entomologist." www.entsoc.org.

swarm of paper wasps in South America. My face swelled up like a balloon. Over the years I have been bitten and stung by a variety of spiders, scorpions and insects; it's an occupational hazard."[42]

Forensic entomologists, on the other hand, deal with working conditions that can be emotionally stressful. Whether doing research or helping solve crimes, they must work with animal and human cadavers, collecting insect specimens from the bodies and exploring the rate of decay that attracts different insects at different times. Natalie K. Lindgren is a graduate student in entomology at the Southeast Texas Applied Forensic Science Facility. She explains that cadaver research takes some getting used to. "My concerns about working with cadavers quickly went away when I realized for us, the researchers, there is no sadness associated with these dead people," she says. "These people or their families donated their bodies because they wanted them to be used for education, training, and research, so to fulfill their wishes we should all try to do the best science that we can."[43] All forensic entomologists must approach their work like Lindgren does and think about the value of their investigations rather than the grief of death.

Personal Qualities

Above all, an entomologist is a scientist and needs to have strong scientific interests and talents. He or she must be able to be objective, be an excellent observer, and be curious, patient, and a critical thinker. Many entomologists also report being interested from a young age in the natural world, insects, and bugs of all sorts. "I still have my boyhood interest in bugs," says entomologist Todd Reichardt. "It's a fascination. I still can't believe how intricate insects look."[44] At the same time, entomologists have to have excellent communication and writing skills because they need to tell others about their discoveries and report the results of their latest research.

What Is the Future Outlook for Entomologists?

For all biological scientists, the Bureau of Labor Statistics predicts a strong job demand and a 20 percent increase in job growth by 2018. Entomologists, especially those who have graduate degrees and certification, can expect to be in high demand, with the same 20 percent rate of job growth.

Asking the Big Questions

"Why are there around 40,000 species of leaf beetles? Why are there 10,000 bird species in the world, or 5,500 mammals? Why was evolution so uneven that some groups became huge and some groups are small? . . . The world outside looks the way it does largely due to beetles. Flowers evolved because of beetles. So my attraction to them is this extraordinary diversity and what are the factors that lead to this diversity."

—Caroline Chaboo, entomologist specializing in leaf beetles

Quoted in Shreya Dasgupta, "A Forest Full of Beetles: An Interview with Bug Researcher Caroline Chaboo," Mongabay, March 1, 2016. https://news.mongabay.com.

Find Out More

Ask an Entomologist
website: https://askentomologists.com

This website was created by a group of entomologists who answer questions about entomology from the public. Anyone can submit a question about any entomology topic, and one of the scientists will answer. You can also read questions submitted by others and learn what the entomologists have to say.

Bug Chicks
website: http://thebugchicks.com

The Bug Chicks are two female entomologists who educate people about the wonderful world of bugs. At their website, you can learn about their research, educational opportunities, and the ways that entomologists study insects. Many articles about insects and related arthropods are available, along with videos about bugs and studying bugs.

Entomological Foundation
3 Park Place, Suite 307
Annapolis, MD 21401
website: www.entfdn.org

The foundation is closely aligned with the Entomological Society of America, but its primary focus is on education of the next generation of scientists and entomologists. At its website, click the link for Kids and find tips, activities, and information for all different age levels. At the high school level, you can access suggestions about colleges offering entomology courses and about age- and interest-appropriate organizations to explore.

Entomological Society of America (ESA)
3 Park Place, Suite 307
Annapolis, MD 21401
website: www.entsoc.org

The ESA is a nonprofit, professional organization dedicated to the advancement of the science of entomology. Some of its benefits are for members only, but anyone can access much of the information on its website. You can read articles and interviews about entomologists and their profession, as well as a section on careers in the discipline and volunteer opportunities for those interested in entomology.

Insects.org
website: www.insects.org

If you are fascinated by insects, this is the website for you. Visitors can read about the importance of insects, learn about insect lives, and see amazing photographs of some beautifully complex bugs. You also can view articles from the organization's *Cultural Entomology Digest*, which explores how insects affect human culture.

SOURCE NOTES

Introduction: For the Love of Animals

1. Molly Goldston, "A Day in the Life of Saving Grace by Molly," *Saving Grace Animals for Adoption Newsletter*, August 17, 2016.
2. Molly Goldston, "Why Am I Still Here?," About Saving Grace, Saving Grace Animals for Adoption, 2010. http://savinggracenc.org.
3. Quoted in Michele C. Hollow, "Qualities for Working with Animals?," Dogtime, 2017. http://dogtime.com.

Wildlife Rehabilitator

4. National Wildlife Rehabilitators Association, "What Is Wildlife Rehabilitation?," 2015. www.nwrawildlife.org.
5. Quoted in *Nature*, "Interview: Julie Anne Collier, Raptor Rehabilitator," PBS, May 1, 2008. www.pbs.org.
6. Quoted in Korrie Edwards, "Interview with Amanda Margraves: Head Wildlife Rehabilitator," Green Mind Initiative, June 5, 2015. https://thegreenmindinitiative.wordpress.com.
7. Quoted in Nicole Ridgway, "24 Hours with a Wildlife Rehabilitator," CNNMoney, 2017. http://money.cnn.com.

Veterinarian

8. Maegan Melillo, "A Day in the Life of a Veterinarian," Clappison Animal Hospital, October 27, 2014. www.clappisonvet.com.
9. Melillo, "A Day in the Life of a Veterinarian."
10. Melillo, "A Day in the Life of a Veterinarian."
11. Quoted in Tom Knapp, "A Day in the Life of a Large-Animal Veterinarian," *Lancaster Online*, September 29, 2013. http://lancasteronline.com.
12. Charles Dolin, "A Day in the Life of a Veterinarian," *Our Blog*, Essex Animal Hospital, October 10, 2012. http://essexanimalhospital.com.

Veterinary Technician

13. Marty Becker, "Time to Sing Out for Vet Techs, the Unsung Heroes of Animal Care," Vetstreet, October 17, 2012. www.vetstreet.com.
14. Marty Becker, "A Vet Gives Thanks for Veterinary Nurses," Vetstreet, October 10, 2016. www.vetstreet.com.

15. Quoted in Jen Reeder, "A Day in the Life of a Veterinary Technician," *Pets Matter* (blog), American Animal Hospital Association, September 20, 2016. www.aaha.org.

16. Quoted in Reeder, "A Day in the Life of a Veterinary Technician."

17. Quoted in Melissa Chichester, "A Day in the Life of a Vet Tech," *Healthy Perspectives* (blog), September 23, 2015. http://blog.puri tan.com.

18. Joey Bryant, "How to Become a Vet Tech," Inner Body, December 20, 2016. www.innerbody.com.

19. Quoted in Vet Tech Career Guide, "Interview with a Veterinary Technician," August 19, 2011. www.veterinary-technician.net.

Pet Groomer

20. Vickie Haywood, "Dog Groomer Insight, A Day in the Life of . . . ," *Dog Press*, April, 2016. www.thedogpress.com.

21. Quoted in Dog Guide, "Interview with a Professional Dog Groomer." www.dogguide.net.

22. Quoted in Arielle Pardes, "12 Things I Wish I Knew Before I Became a Dog Groomer," *Cosmopolitan*, June 7, 2016. www.cosmopolitan .com.

23. Ellen Ehrlich, "Life Lessons of Pet Grooming," *Groomer to Groomer*, May 14, 2015. www.groomertogroomer.com.

Farrier

24. Leigh Ballard, "A Day in the Life of a Farrier," *Mid-South Horse Review*, July 6, 2012. www.midsouthhorsereview.com.

25. Quoted in EHUK News, "A Day in the Life of a Farrier," *Everything Horse*, August 12, 2016. http://everythinghorseuk.co.uk.

26. Quoted in Rachel Sauer, "Horse Play: Brian Crandall Enjoys Life as Farrier, Horseshoe Artist," *Grand Junction (CO) Daily Sentinel*, March 6, 2015. www.gjsentinel.com.

27. John Suttle, "Hoofcare Business Strategy—Take Charge of Your Business," Successful Farrier. http://successfulfarrier.com.

28. Quoted in Editor, "How to Make It in a Career as a Farrier: Q&A with Mark Plumlee," Farrier Guide, May 7, 2013. www.thefarrierguide .com.

Fish and Game Warden

29. Quoted in Teresa Mioli, "A Day in the Life of a Game Warden," *Beaumont (TX) Enterprise*, January 6, 2010. www.beaumontenterprise .com.

30. Quoted in Shmoop, "Game Warden: Typical Day," 2017. www.shmoop.com.
31. Quoted in College Foundation of North Carolina, "Conservation Officer: Interviews," CFNC.org. www.cfnc.org.
32. Quoted in David Hagengruber, "Game Warden 'Glamour,'" *Montana Outdoors*, September/October 2004. http://fwp.mt.gov.
33. Quoted in College Foundation of North Carolina, "Conservation Officer."
34. Quoted in College Foundation of North Carolina, "Conservation Officer."

Primatologist

35. Quoted in Allison Forsythe, "What Does a Canadian Primatologist Do?," Jane Goodall Institute of Canada, September 5, 2013. http://janegoodall.ca.
36. Bethan J. Morgan, "Notes from the Field: A Primatologist's Point of View," Nature Education Knowledge Project, Scitable, 2012. www.nature.com.
37. Kevin Hunt, "Careers in Field Work," Primate Info Net, 2013. http://pin.primate.wisc.edu.
38. Quoted in Kristi Foster, "The Pros (and Cons) of Being a Primatologist —Part 1," Conservation Careers, December 31, 2015. www.conservation-careers.com.
39. Hunt, "Careers in Field Work."

Entomologist

40. Nina Stanczyk, "A Day in the Life of an Entomologist," *Wellcome Collection Blog*, April 15, 2013. https://blog.wellcomecollection.org.
41. Stanczyk, "A Day in the Life of an Entomologist."
42. Quoted in Debbie Glade, "Educating the World One Creepy Crawly at a Time: An Interview with Author & Entomologist George McGavin, PhD," Smart Books for Smart Kids, March 17, 2014. www.smartbooksforsmartkids.com.
43. Quoted in Entomology Today, "Forensic Entomology Is More than Just Blow Flies and Beetles," January 22, 2015. https://entomologytoday.org.
44. Quoted in College Foundation of North Carolina, "Entomologist: Interviews," CFNC.org. www.cfnc.org.

INTERVIEW WITH A VETERINARY TECHNICIAN

Tammy Shumaker is a veterinary technician with Blackstone Animal Clinic in Blackstone, Virginia. She has worked as a vet tech for twenty-one years. She answered questions about her career by e-mail.

Q: Why did you become a veterinary technician?

A: Well, I originally never wanted to be a vet tech. I always wanted to be a veterinarian. But as life and chance would happen, or in this case not happen, I became a technician. For vet school, you have to have a lot of working hours under a veterinarian. So I started working at an animal hospital after I received my bachelors in biology. All the while, I was sending in applications to vet schools and then going on to get my Masters as well. Of course, after many years of desperately trying, I did not get in. But during all of this time, I realized that the hands-on day-to-day interaction with the animals happens more with the technicians than the doctors. The doctors do their exams and evaluations of illnesses/wellness. But the actual caretaking is definitely by the technician. So I continued to stay in the field because I knew I wanted to help the animals as much as I could.

Q: Can you describe your typical workday?

A: My day usually starts doing the treatments and medicines for the previous day's hospitalized animals. This includes checking on all of the previous day surgeries—if their incisions are healing, if they are eating and drinking, if they have a fever, making sure they get their meds, and getting an overall idea of each animal's wellness. Then the hospitalized or sick pets need their treatments, which may include oral medicine, injections, subcutaneous (under the skin) fluids, or repeating any blood work that the doctor may have requested. All the while, we will also be seeing appointments. That is, assisting the doctor in treating the patients, putting charges in the computer, making up oral medicines to go home.

Then we may have surgeries as well. For these we need to calculate anesthetic drugs and make preparations for the doctor, which include making sure all the instruments needed are there, having their surgery suite ready to go for whatever surgery is scheduled, prepping the surgery site prior to surgery, and then assisting the doctors during the procedure to monitor the anesthesia. Then you will monitor the patient until they have recovered from surgery. Some days we may have dental procedures as well, and I am able to scale and polish teeth. We will end on more appointments and also send home any patients that may need to go home. The last part of the day is to do any evening treatments that any hospitalized pets may have and to make sure every patient in the hospital is taken care of before they are left alone.

Q: What do you like most about your job?

A: What I enjoy the most is seeing the patients heal and make full recoveries from their illnesses. Seeing them go back to their owners happy and healthy gives my heart joy. And to know that you might have made the difference gives meaning to your job.

Q: What do you like least about your job?

A: Euthanasia. In this field, it's not all puppies, kittens, and rainbows like a lot of people think. There's animal cruelty that you wish your eyes and mind could undo. There's illnesses that you cannot always fix even with all the money and specialists in the field. This means you cannot save someone's beloved pet.

And the worst thing in the world is to have to watch an owner make the horrible decision to euthanize their pet because it's the right thing to do. It's absolutely heartbreaking. But it's also the ultimate gift to give to that pet to not have to suffer anymore. And the owners that are able to stay with their pets through the procedure give the ultimate respect to them, too. Because in the beginning

75

our pets just give love to us unconditionally and ask for nothing in return. So during this procedure, the owner returns that love by staying with them to the last breath. It's hard to watch but it's one of the most loving moments you will ever be a part of.

Q: What personal qualities do you find most valuable for this type of work?

A: Two things come to mind that are a sure requirement: caretaking and empathy. Now of course, there are a lot of things that you should have to do this job. Things like being good in math, being physically strong, and just being a hard worker. But these are things most jobs require. Caretaking cannot be taught. You know if it is in your nature. You may not have this skill for everything in life; I certainly do not get that feeling working on people. But the kind, tender spirit in animals touches my heart. Just how they look to you for help even when they can't tell you what's wrong inside. They just trust you to make them better.

The other thing is empathy. You have to be able to understand the pet's and the owner's feelings. You need to feel their love and their sadness. It makes you a better technician and a better human. I have always said that the day a euthanasia didn't make me shed a tear or affect me, then I don't need to do this job anymore.

Q: What advice do you have for students who might be interested in this career?

A: I have been doing this job for almost twenty-one years and I still love it. It's hard, it has long hours, and you're not going to be rich by any means. But at the end of the day, you do feel like you have accomplished something. You have helped give a longer and healthier life to something that otherwise could not help itself. Very rewarding!

OTHER CAREERS IF YOU LIKE ANIMALS

Animal control officer
Animal cruelty investigator
Animal photographer
Animal trainer
Apiarist
Aquarist
Dairy farm owner
Dog day care provider
Dog handler
Ecologist
Ethologist
Guide dog trainer
Habitat specialist
Herpetologist
Horse groom
Horse rancher
Horse trainer

Ichthyologist
Marine biologist
Microbiologist
Naturalist/wildlife biologist
Ornithologist
Park naturalist
Pet portrait artist
Pet sitter
Ranch manager
Reptile farmer
Rescue sanctuary manager
State animal health inspector
Veterinary acupuncturist
Veterinary assistant
Zoo curator
Zookeeper
Zoologist

Editor's note: The online *Occupational Outlook Handbook* of the US Department of Labor's Bureau of Labor Statistics is an excellent source of information on jobs in hundreds of career fields, including many of those listed here. The *Occupational Outlook Handbook* may be accessed online at www.bls.gov/ooh.

INDEX